Contents

Session material

What is Messy Church?

Messy Church is a form of church for all ages together that involves creativity, celebration and hospitality. Church, but not as you know it!

What are its values?

Christ-centred

All Age

Celebration

Creativity

Hospitality

What's involved?

A Messy Church usually meets once a month and includes four sections:

- **Welcome:** a warm welcome.
- **Activities:** An hour of fun interactive activities exploring the biblical theme.
- **Celebration:** a short gathered time with story, song and prayer.
- **Meal:** A sit-down meal for everyone.

Go to **messychurch.org.uk/getmessymay21** to download all templates at A4 size, including a session planning sheet.

If you are using these sessions for a Messy Church at home, look out for this symbol! These are activities that can easily be adapted to the home.

In our next issue

SEPTEMBER Trusting is believing

OCTOBER Alone and scared

NOVEMBER Sew miraculous!

DECEMBER The birth of Jesus

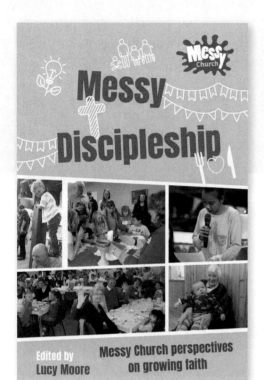

Messy Discipleship

As the fastest-growing fresh expression of church in the UK, Messy Church has learnt a thing or two about discipleship since its beginnings in 2004, but if 2020 taught us anything, it's that we still have much to learn. A new book, Messy Discipleship, gathers together what we know so far.

This collection of perspectives, edited by Lucy Moore, brings academic analysis and practitioner wisdom to bear on a key question for today's church, capturing the latest thinking and learning from the Messy Church context. Explore individual chapters examining each of the core Messy Church values and how these work in practice to promote discipleship.

Whether 2020 was a challenging year for discipleship in your community, or your Messy Church flourished as you learnt new ways to be disciples, find your refresher on discipleship at brfonline.org.uk/messydiscipleship.

The longer I spend marvelling at the goings-on in the world of Messy Church, the more I'm convinced that discipleship has less to do with a single glamorous or feel-good experience and much more to do with obedience, attitude, under-the-surface 'heart' stuff, perseverance, resilience, dogged determination, single-minded (bloody-minded, even) unstoppableness in a journey towards, with and from Jesus. ('From' because it all starts with him.)

Lucy Moore, from the introduction to *Messy Discipleship*

Order at brfonline.org.uk

Lucy Moore writes...
Sowing in tears

I've cried a lot over the last year, as I expect many of us have. I'd like to claim that it's been because of the national and global crisis that's traumatised us all at such a profound level – and indeed, some of the tears were for that reason. It's been miserable for old and young and in-betweeners. Many of us knew the loving and energetic Julie Quantrill in Aberdeenshire, who threw herself with so much commitment and generosity into her Messy Church ministry as well as many other ways of helping people know Jesus. We were devastated to hear of her sudden illness in 2020 and miss her so much. With so many attacks from so many directions, I wondered whether this was the moment when Messy Church would go under and never resurface. 'Record my misery; list my tears on your scroll – are they not in your record?' groans the psalmist in Psalm 56:8 (NIV).

But as the months pass and the devastation of 2020 and early 2021 has given way to a new year and new opportunities, we can see the rhythm of the seasons being worked out, like the faith expressed in Psalm 126:5–6: 'Those who sow with tears will reap with songs of joy. Those who go out weeping, carrying seed to sow, will return with songs of joy, carrying sheaves with them.' It's particularly striking as an image as, this year, we're thinking so much about ways Messy Churches can be in touch with the things of the earth. Planting seeds, acorns and bulbs is very much at the forefront of our minds. We've all enjoyed planting into pots with Messy families – a good muddy, messy activity, always surrounded with laughter, smiles of achievement and the sense of creating something real to look forward to as the plant grows.

The thought of sowing those sunflower seeds with tears pouring down our faces, or of wretchedly sprinkling cress seeds on to paper towels in despair, just feels wrong. Sowing should be a time of hope for what is to come.

> 'Those who sow with tears will reap with songs of joy.'
> Psalm 126:5

The Messy Church sowing during 2020 – as we reimagined Messy Church for the new situation – was often done with tears in our eyes. But perhaps now we're seeing hope rising again. God's faithfulness has held us through it all so far. **YOUR faithfulness** to the families in your Messy Church and **YOUR determination** to keep on sowing in the expectation of a harvest, even when it's had to be done in metaphorical sleet, with a broken tractor and, as it were, gremlins rising from the soil to attack your ankles – **YOUR commitment** has been part of the reason Messy Church is making it through. You've stayed connected and you've encouraged those around you. You've shared ideas, resources and skills. You've been vulnerable and said what isn't working as well as what is. You've believed enough in the values to want to reimagine them, rather than take the easy option and abandon them. Some have even started new Messy Churches! We're still enjoying the connectivity of Facebook Lives on a Wednesday, thanks to the generosity of so many friends. Some of these too have helped us take steps to come closer to the created world – remember Rachel Summers and Wild Worship? Or Benjamin Carter and God's tent? Or Sandy Brodine out in the wilderness of Australia?

The pattern of the seasons is one of death to life, just as the rhythm of our life in Jesus reflects his death and resurrection life. As the lover says in the ancient poem:

> *See! The winter is past; the rains are over and gone,*
> *Flowers appear on the earth; the season of singing*
> * has come,*
> *the cooing of doves is heard in our land.*
> *The fig-tree forms its early fruit; the blossoming vines*
> * spread their fragrance.*
> **Song of Solomon 2:11–13 (NIV)**

When we're watching for God in whichever season of the natural world we're in around the world, let's look for those signs of life and hope.

The Netherlands

Kliederkerk: hope within chaos

Nelleke Plomp

'We all could use a smile in these times of Covid… and that happened! Today for the first time since March we had a kliederkerk with "The good life" as theme.' This Facebook post, with a lot of colourful pictures, summarises perfectly the feeling of a lot of kliederkerk teams.

After half a year of 'intelligent lockdown', with minimum possibilities to gather as communities, we see glimpses of hope. Kliederkerken are finding creative ways to come together, to discover a Bible story and to celebrate together. Some have even found ways to eat together within the boundaries of the restrictions. It is amazing to see children, parents, grandparents, neighbours of all ages, personalities and backgrounds having fun together. But we see also a lot of teams who – understandably – haven't started up again. As a national team, we provided tips, a few 'kliederkerk at home'

programmes and booklets for families. Local teams used those to support their members. Some delivered nice little kliederkerk packages to the homes; some provided online meetings.

Recently, we created a few complete and corona-compliant sessions. Hopefully they will make it easy for the 180 kliederkerk teams to join together.

Lastly, one of the most beautiful lessons I learned working for kliederkerk is that God is present within the chaos and even makes something beautiful out of chaos. Yes, there is Covid, unsure times and chaos, but God is there! How hopeful is that!

Sweden

Messy Church outdoors

Gudrun Grunnesjö and Katarina Pettersson

In the parish of Hudiksvall we have seen Messy Church grow these last two years in many ways. What started with some families has now spread to include many more. Many enjoy the big community of people from all generations, backgrounds and nationalities, all in one lovely mess. The celebration times give the most joy of all. They make you long for more. Sharing, community, joy, peace in the presence of the Lord and simplicity are all things we have experienced and heard many talk about as very important.

In these coronavirus times we have tried to have Messy Church outdoors. We have specifically invited families who might be new to church. We meet on Saturdays at 11 am and start with some singing practice and Bible reading. Then families go together to different stations. We have a time of celebration together and finish with a packed lunch.

The first theme was the feeding of the 5,000. We baked bread over an open fire, made fish from items found in nature, visited a fishpond and crafted fish.

The second theme was Zacchaeus. Everyone started with walking through the gates of Jericho and got to meet Zacchaeus. Then they climbed trees like Zacchaeus did, made stilts from upturned pots to become taller, crawled into a small playhouse to find balls to throw and much more. We had the celebration with drama outdoors. Both times we have tried to stick to our normal Messy Church celebration form: we have a procession song, we light candles, make the cross sign, sing our special song with a dance, have a short creative sermon, pray and have lots of movements in all we do, including the songs.

To be outdoors works really well but we do long to have Messy Church in the real way again soon.

New Zealand

Drive-through takeaway Messy Church

Mary Addison

In September we held a drive-through takeaway Messy Church as we still couldn't meet together. The families loved it. The outside of the church was decorated with paper lanterns and bunting. We provided a takeaway meal for each family. They had had to register with me a few days earlier so we knew what to prepare. We gave each family a homemade lasagne in a tinfoil dish, a container of coleslaw plus dressing, a loaf of bread and a two-litre container of ice cream and sprinkles to go on the ice cream,. The theme was 'You are God's Treasure'. I staggered arrival times over an hour and a half and kept people in their bubbles when they arrived. Just three of us (my core team) did the cooking for over 100 people, and mainly prepared the takeaway bags. We held a treasure hunt on our church road, which the families explored to answer the questions and get their treasure (a small chocolate bar) when they arrived back with it all filled in. They all stayed in their family bubble doing the treasure hunt. Coloured glass pebbles had been left along the trail for the children to find. When

they returned, they put one of them with their initials on it in our treasure box as a prayer offering that was blessed in church the next day. Families then drove up to church and picked up their bag and meal box. Lots of horn honking and laughter. Everyone had fun and enjoyed themselves without coming into the church building and we were able to meet the Covid regulations.

This Messy Church proved to be our biggest with us connecting with well over 120 people, even without 20 of our team being involved. Our local Adult Mental Health Home took part. They love coming to Messy Church, where their messy lives are accepted as the norm. The home then cooked lasagne for the 20 residents' tea so we didn't have to prepare their food. They took individual MC bags of activities back to the Home to complete.

Germany

Kirche Kunterbunt

Damaris Binder

'Kirche Kunterbunt' ('motley church') – the German version of Messy Church – is currently writing a roaring success story. All our online seminars, and the live ones, where permitted to be held, are fully booked. On average, two new Kirche Kunterbunts register on our website every month – in spite of the coronavirus. This is immensely encouraging and hopeful.

groups went on to the next activity point.

Several workshops on various topics were later offered, such as how to be more all-age, starting a Kirche Kunterbunt, science in Kirche Kunterbunt and many more.

On 3 October 2020, we organised a Kirche Kunterbunt inspiration day – with masks, sanitiser and distancing to enable as many participants as possible to enjoy the programme. Due to the coronavirus, we offered the programme twice. Thus, about 100 participants received information on Kirche Kunterbunt and – even more importantly – experienced it live.

The focus was on Kirche Kunterbunt values: hospitality, all-age, celebration, creativity, Christ-centred. The participants experienced these values during the activity time in fixed groups, having eight minutes per activity. The activity points were arranged in a one-way street in order to avoid congestion and keep up the social distancing. When a noise sounded, the

Dr Dave, Messy Science Coordinator, participated in person and contributed elephant toothpaste to the celebration time, which was a special highlight. In spite of not being able to sing in fellowship, we still had a cheerful and positive day. Many participants returned home grateful and inspired, and will hopefully start their own Kirche Kunterbunt.

Finland

Messy Church in Finland

Liisa Kuusela

Greetings from Messy Church in Turku, Finland. We have run Messy Church for around two years in Turku, which is one of the biggest cities in Finland. Everything started, from my perspective, in Messy Church in St Andrew's Church in London. During the springtime 2018 I spent three months as a visiting pastor around that area. And when I heard about Messy Church I immediately thought, 'Is this the reason why God sent me to London?' Now I surely know it was.

As a Lutheran Church we also need new fresh ways to get families to join the church. Messy Church has started very well. It was very easy to get a team which consists of both women and men, young people and older ones. Many of them are volunteers, with two church staff: me and our family worker. The Church Council understood straight away that this is something we need to start. So we got funding.

We have Messy Church once a month (of course, we had to cancel Messy Church a couple of times during the pandemic) on Sunday afternoons. We meet in a cosy old vicarage which has a very nice garden. This allows us to arrange some activities outside which is good, especially for lively children.

We also host confirmation classes at Messy Church.

We are so grateful to God that he has blessed our Messy Church. The challenge at the moment is to also get older people to join the Messy Church.

The story of Messy Church is growing around Finland. Already now there are at least two Messy Churches in Helsinki (our capital) area. It's great!

Canada

Covid-creative Canadian Messy Church

Carol Fletcher

What began as an exciting year of 2020 quickly became the all-too-familiar Covid-confounded 2020.

Messy Church Canada planned for a national conference in October 2020 and we looked forward to welcoming international and national guests to Winnipeg.

Messy Church Canada was like a ship in full sail – growing congregations, exciting possibilities and more.

But 2020 was like an unwelcome wind and it was determined to blow us right off course. By God's grace, Messy Church Canada was also like a house built on rock, not on sand, and we were not blown over.

From coast to coast to coast (yes – we have three coasts) and across all six time zones, Messy Churches have moved to Messy Church in a bag, or Messy Church at home. Certainly, some

leadership teams have been stretched so far that they are taking a break, while others are flourishing creatively.

As we move into 2021 we are hopeful for many things. I expect that when you read this, it will be a different time than when I am writing. We look forward to days without curfews and limits on gathering. We look forward to a national conference and the international one! We look forward to the blessings of Zoom and the gifts of technology that help us to declare that God is here, God is there, God is completely everywhere.

We are not alone, we live in God's world, thanks be to God.

Meet our new Messy Church Coordinator

Lucy Moore

We are rampant traditionalists in Messy Church and simply can't face the thought of being down on our quota of Janes. So it is with huge delight that we welcome our newest member of the BRF team, the new Messy Church Coordinator, the lovely **Jane Butler**. There were incredibly strong candidates for the role – frankly, we were spoiled for choice at interview and wanted to appoint everyone. Jane impressed us with her formidable admin skills, tech skills, people skills, but even more with her deep-seated passion for and calling to Messy Church, a passion that will enrich and bless us all as we work out how to sing the Lord's song in this strange Covid-ridden land.

Jane is from Nottingham and is part of the Messy Church team at Toton. She's been working for Boots in IT and supporting her local Messy Church in her spare time, as many of us do, so she knows what it's like at the coalface. Glitterface. Pastaface. Bagface. Whatever.

Her new role is a three-day-a-week heady cocktail of developing and maintaining the structures so that our new support teams can be as free as possible to support Messy Churches on the ground where it matters, along with cheering everyone on, keeping all our creativity within the bounds of reality and enabling us to do far more than we could do without her expertise.

The main problem is what to call her – 'Messy Jane' is taken, as is 'Jane B', as another wonderful Jane (Butcher) works more closely with us in her new role: 'New Jane' would only work for the first month, 'Techie Jane' might be misread as 'Tetchy Jane', which is far from the truth… it's a puzzle. Never mind! The great thing is that God has sent us someone with the gifts we need for this new season. Do pray for Jane – pray for all the Janes! – as she settles into her new role and helps us all grow the kingdom of heaven even more effectively in our Messy ministry. You can contact her at **jane.butler@brf.org.uk**.

Sustainable Messy Church

Jean Pienaar

'All we have to do is wake up and change.'
Greta Thunberg

Sustainability has become increasingly topical in the last few decades as we have begun to see the impact of our consumerist lifestyles. Some people have made radical lifestyle changes, while others have considered it fake news and continued with their greedy behaviour. Sustainability is concerned not only with the state of the natural world, but also with poverty, population growth, gender equality, indigenous issues, peace and reconciliation, community life and human health. All these things are interconnected. It is important how we live our lives now and into the future.

As stewards of God's creation, it is critically important for Messy Church to play a role in developing responsible stewardship in our attitude towards our environment, others and ourselves. We also model responsible stewardship to our volunteers and our families in what we do and how we do it. To what extent is Messy Church eco-friendly?

Do we use locally sourced (and renewable) materials? Not only is this generally cost-efficient, but we learn to appreciate what we have around us. Messy Church people are generally good at using recyclable household items (how many different uses are there for an empty loo roll?!) and adapting the crafts and activities to materials that are accessible and available. Pasta can be an eco-alternative to plastic straws, and tea or coffee an alternative to paint. Do we recycle craft materials that haven't been used?

Do we use locally sourced and seasonal food? How do we ensure that food isn't wasted? What do we do with leftover food? Are there some people who live on the street who would enjoy the last bit of mac and cheese that the teenagers haven't polished off? Are there composting facilities available?

We increase our knowledge through learning, experience, action and participation. How can Messy Church not only impart knowledge and offer experiences, but also be an agent of sustainability and a steward of God's creation through action and participation?

A new season of support

Lucy Moore

Frankly, we all need all the support we can get at the moment! As you probably know, the last year has made us rethink the way we offer support to Messy Churches in the UK. We came up with a rather exciting idea, which is based on what Messy Churches need for this season and what the support teams can offer.

I want to start a Messy Church in Little Splodlington. What do I do?
EBENEEZER LEMON

This request will be passed on to a member of the **Green 'Getting Going' team**, who will contact Mr Lemon and find out what is needed. The Green team member will probably recommend that Mr Lemon and co watch the 'Starting a Messy Church' video from the website, if their tech skills allow. Then the Green team member might offer a short Zoom conversation with the team or church council to explain the basics, answer questions, talk through the resources and point them in the right direction.

Our Messy Church team is going through a really tough patch. Please will you pray for us?
Rapunzel Treadmill

BRF will pass on the request to the **Gold 'Prayer' team**, who have a special calling to prayer and will communicate this need among the team, as anonymously and sensitively as requested. BRF can assure Rapunzel that her team will be surrounded by prayer and love and that she is not alone.

Our Messy Church is five years old and we need a bit of a boost.
Gertrude Fendickerty

BRF will pass this request to a member of the **Purple 'Alongsiders' team**. The Purple team member will get in touch with Gertrude and they will decide together what the best support might be. It could be just one Zoom to remind the team what it's all about, or it might be an offer to accompany Gertrude's team over a few months in a short-term online learning community, to help them find a new purpose and intentionality. It will be like having a critical friend or Messy coach offering you a friendly listening ear and asking helpful questions.

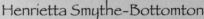

I'd like a training session for my team on discipleship in Messy Church.
Henrietta Smythe-Bottomton

There's an obvious grey area here between what the **Purple team** offers and what the **Red 'Trainers' team** offers, but the BRF office will sort out which team can offer the most effective help. If the need is more for training than accompanying, BRF will make two suggestions. Either Henrietta might book her team onto one of the scheduled training sessions advertised on the Messy Church website. Or she might book a private session just for her team. In both situations, the **Red team** is the one that delivers. They will be delivering regular scheduled online training throughout the year for anyone to book into. They will also be available to deliver the private sessions. It will all be online for the moment anyway, so a Red trainer in Scotland might lead a training session with another **Red team** member from Cornwall for a church in Lincolnshire: all very exciting!

It's Bible Sunday next month and we would love someone to talk about the work of BRF at our online church service, as we want to make a donation to the work of Messy Church.

Javad Faizal, Treasurer of St Winstanley's

BRF will pass this request to someone on the **Orange 'Advocates' team**. The **Orange team**'s role is to be *au fait* with all that's going on at BRF, not just Messy Church, and the team will be in close contact with Jane Butcher, the BRF Volunteer Lead, who will make sure they have all the information they need to do a great job. If the **Orange team** can tear themselves away from their latest plan for raising funds for Messy Church, one of them will deliver a splendid talk for Javad's church.

I've written 250 sessions for Messy Churches on the theme of the mortification of the flesh. Please will you share them with the network?

Tobias Entwhistle

BRF will pass Tobias' generous offering to a member of the **Pink 'Writers and Readers' team**, who will be able to suggest to BRF whether or not it would indeed be a helpful resource to share online, make into a book or reinvent as, for example, a series of videos.

The other teams will be hard at work in different spheres. The **Blue 'Pool of Wisdom' team** is already working on organising the **Messtival** for May this year – they are a pool of people who have wisdom and experience to offer in making things happen in the Messy world. And the **Teal 'Specialists' team** is a collection of people with diverse skills in specific areas or who have a specific geographical remit through their job or their network, who can be called upon to help with requests for help in those areas. The **Silver 'Storykeepers'**

team props Lucy up in her increasing dotage and reminds her what it's all about. And as things develop, we'll be forming new teams for new needs: perhaps a Crimson Comms team? A Turquoise Tech team? A Violet Video team? Time will tell.

Please pray for these teams and for those supporting them – and make use of them! Contact messychurch@brf.org.uk **or explore** messychurch.org.uk/messy-church-teams**.**

Now available

Ten fun-filled sessions!

Edited by Lucy Moore

Messy Church Does Science After-School Club

This pack is for churches who want a tried-and-tested way of contributing to the life of their local school, or for schools who would like to hold an after-school event with the values of Messy Church. Based on *Messy Church Does Science* (BRF, 2017), these ten sessions will help you run an after-school club for families to explore faith questions through science. Each session focuses on two or three science activities, with further ideas for a Bible-based celebration and, if appropriate, a prayer. £9.99 from brfonline.org.uk

Network news

International Conference, 20-22 May 2022
Key international leaders, 23-24 May 2022

Derbyshire, UK

Oh the people you'll meet! Oh the things that you'll do! – not quite Dr Seuss's words, but of that genre. It's only a year till the 2022 Messy Church International Conference, and bookings are open.

It's being planned by an international, intergenerational team and already looks like being a whole lot of unmissably inspirational and educational fun. If 'education' means 'leading you out to broader horizons and new possibilities', the education you'll get from being a delegate will be something quite remarkable. In previous years people have talked about the way the penny dropped for them, while they were at the conference, and how their Messy Church ministry and vocation took a new and dynamic direction. The sense of belonging it brings, the feeling of being part of this worldwide family, of stepping into the slipstream of the Spirit; the cross-fertilisation of ideas over mealtimes and coffee breaks and late into the night: it's a university for the soul. And quite frankly, we would love to spend time with you. Beware – you could end up like the small group of Canadians and Australians who meet every week on Zoom for a glass of wine and a catch-up, after making friends with each other at the conference in 2019!

We'll keep you posted about the speakers, programme items and more on the website over the coming year and we'll have a Facebook group for delegates, to make it easier to suggest shared travel arrangements and to make the most of the opportunities to meet up.

We'll be taking over The Hayes Conference Centre in Swanwick. If you haven't visited Derbyshire before, it's a beautiful county and you may want to keep some time free before and after the conference to visit Chatsworth House, Hardwick Hall, Alton Towers Theme Park or to explore the Peak District, depending on your tastes. The Conference Centre is part of the same organisation as High Leigh, where we've been in previous years, and is a little larger, so we can invite more people, but still keep that personal welcome and friendliness we've enjoyed in the past.

One big development is that we are planning the programme with leaders of all ages in mind. We can't make it a completely all-age conference yet, but if you have younger leaders to bring along, the teenagers on the planning team are making sure that what we plan is fun, relevant and accessible to everyone genuinely interested in making their Messy Church even better. (Please note, the conference will definitely be for team members and not pitched at families who are part of Messy Church but don't help lead it.) Younger team leaders will need to be accompanied by a responsible adult.

The ideas flying around at the moment include a pre-conference pilgrimage in the Peak District (!!!), an international food festival (!!!), Mega Messy Church sessions across three halls simultaneously (!!!), an amazing speaker (???!), workshops on all aspects of Messy Church you could imagine and some you never could, and oh so much more.

For more information and to book, go to messychurch.org.uk/MCIC22

Snapshots from the last Messy Church International Conference, 2019

12 ☐ⓟ☐ @MessyChurchBRF

MESSTIVAL

Book the date!

Can't wait till 2022 for a Messy Church festival gathering? Fear not! (Drum roll) …

We bring you the 2021 UK MESSTIVAL! This May!

Everybody welcome, whether you lead a Messy Church or are a family who goes to one! It's going to be a huge, fun online festival, brought to you by BRF and the Blue team with contributions from the other support teams (see pages 10–11).

The morning is particularly for Messy Church leaders and teams of all ages. The afternoon is a chance for Messy families, plus teams and leaders to join in the biggest online Messy Church EVER! The Guinness Book of Records has been mentioned…

In the morning, it'll be like a festival with fun-and-fact-filled tents to explore (mud entirely optional). First, we'll gather together on Zoom to be warmly welcomed into the day with some unmissable joy from some of our great leaders. Then you can wander off to the different tents – there'll be LOADS of brilliant people offering talks on all things Messy, from hands-on 'how to make a…' to serious stuff about discipleship, the planet or great ways to pray, plus hospitality tents where you can go and hang out with members of the support teams and chat, or arrange to meet Messy friends – 'Why don't we spend the first slot in the Golden Palace of Prayer and ask for God's blessing on our Messy families?' 'See you in Charis' House of Cake in the second slot!' or 'After we've been to two talks, let's talk about it all as a team in Lucy's Tiki Bar!' Bursting with all these new ideas, we'll gather briefly at the end of the morning to be thankful to God in a big gathered Zoomfest.

Then, even more excitingly, in the afternoon, we're inviting YOU to set up a Messy Church locally in your community, in whatever way is best by then – it may need to be Messy Church in a bag or the session delivered to homes, or it may be in bubbles or in an outside space, or socially distanced – but some version of YOUR Messy Church where you live. We'll put the session online as usual for you to download, adapt and share with your families. Picture the same Messy Church activities being done in homes and maybe churches all over the UK, then everyone turning on the computer at 3.00 pm for the YouTube Premiere of the Big Celebration! (And if you can't make it at 3.00 pm, you can watch it later; if you want to watch it and THEN do the activities, that's completely up to you too!)

It'll be Pentecost weekend, so the theme will be great for a family Thy Kingdom Come event.

Head over to messychurch.org.uk/messtival to check out the programme and decide how you'll spend the morning – maybe talk with your team and cover as many tents as possible between you.

It's free to join in with, but we would love to raise money for BRF through donations, so please give even a tiny amount when you book in.

Book the date: Saturday 22 May

Book the time: 10.00 am–12.30 pm for the morning Messtival and whatever time suits you in the afternoon, with the Messtival celebration premiering at 3.00.

Book your bubble: get some friends round! Depending on restrictions, you could get in food and craft supplies and invite a number of people to your home or church hall to join in the morning and afternoon together, or you could join in on your own.

The whole idea of only holding the International Conference every three years was to allow space for other countries to hold their own conferences in the intervening years – so we thought we would hold one specially for the UK, especially for people who can't make it to the international one in 2022. I expect a few of our overseas friends will sneak in and they will be VERY WELCOME too!

#discipleship: team

Messy Adventure

Do you remember, during lockdown we galloped round the world on the Messy Adventure, sharing journey stories from the Bible and visiting some amazing spots across four continents? You can find the videos on the Messy Adventure playlist on the Messy Church YouTube channel.

This year we want to have another Messy Adventure but not for Ascension – for Advent instead, an Advent Adventure with the theme **Joy to the world!** Starting on Sunday 28 November, we want to feature a joyful 'thing' from a Messy Church somewhere in the world every day of Advent. It could be a photo, a very short video (30 seconds max), a short song, a cartoon… something you or your Messy Church have made and that we can share online, one a day, to celebrate Jesus bringing joy to the world where you are.

It's early, but start thinking now if you might send something in from your Messy Church. Picture a gloomy, tired, depressed person glancing at Facebook, Twitter or Instagram at the start of a grey December day and clicking by mistake on your message – what would make that person break into a smile and feel the world is a better place? More details coming soon…

Joy to the world!

Messy Vintage: the book

Messy Vintage is Christ-centred and creative, full of celebration and hospitality and open to all, aspiring to include people of all ages while specifically reaching out to older people. A typical session involves hands-on creative activities to explore a Bible story, a short celebration with story, song and prayer, and refreshments.

Whether you're just getting started with Messy Vintage or looking for new session material, this book offers practical advice and resources to help you reach out to the older people in your community. £8.99 from **brfonline.org.uk**

'A wonderful resource book for Messy Vintage leaders written with Katie and Jill's warm friendliness and expertise. It's so exciting to see this ministry among older people flourishing, and this book will help even more churches join in.'
Lucy Moore, Messy Church founder and pioneer

'The Messy Vintage team always make me feel welcome – they are worth their weight in gold.'
Messy Vintage participant

'We love Messy Vintage. It's like a breath of fresh air!'
Care home social activities coordinator

Messy Vintage
52 sessions to share Christ-centred fun and fellowship with the older generation

Katie Norman and Jill Phipps

Messy Vintage

Jill Phipps

I write this on a dull and cold day in early December, made brighter by the news that a Covid vaccine is literally just around the corner, and that care home residents and staff, and those over 80, will be near the top of the queue to receive it. This is great news for Messy Vintage groups, most of whom have not met face to face for the past nine months.

However, much has been going on, in spite of the difficulties. Whether in the community or in care homes, older people and the staff who care for them have been supported and encouraged and remembered in prayer. Several of the BRF Anna Chaplaincy strategy team wrote and, with the marvellous BRF publishing team, produced five booklets to support care staff in their work. These include tips on how to look after yourself in stressful times and help in leading worship with individual residents or with a group (**brfonline.org.uk/carersguides**). These are a valuable resource, as activity coordinators have suddenly had to become worship leaders as well.

One successful service that I sent in to one of my care homes was adapted from a Godly Play session written specifically for children in the autumn term. It focused on the story of Noah's Ark, written from Noah's wife's point of view (how much longer she could keep the lions from eating the zebras), and thinking about the good, and not so good, things about being stuck indoors with your family (or the same set of people) for a long time. It prompted discussion on what we are grateful for and what we hope for in the future. The rainbow is God's promise of hope – the promise that he is always with us, whatever situation we find ourselves in, and whatever 2021 brings!

Parenting for Faith

Becky Sedgwick

I was reading the parable of the talents, when I suddenly found myself wondering: maybe the third servant wasn't really lazy at all? He might have been the most brilliant gardener ever, but just hopeless with money. So when the master handed him the bag of cash, he simply pushed it under his mattress and buried his head in the sand.

It's all about putting people in the right places to use the particular talents that God's given them – something Messy Church leaders are really good at, drawing in all sorts of people, from Bob who loves astronomy to help with some stargazing, to young Ellen and her amazing prayer activities, and to Margaret, whose pastoral heart just oozes with love for the mums she chats to.

At Parenting for Faith, we love to encourage parents and carers that their children, however young, have purpose and are needed as part of the body of Christ.

But we can be quick to dismiss what we do. 'I just help in the kitchen'; 'I just do the PowerPoint'; 'I just clean up.' One of the ways to help anyone (young or old) recognise how the things they do are vital to God's plan is to show them the impact of what they do. So to Mavis in the kitchen you might say: 'Those friendly words you say as you pour the tea make newcomers feel so welcome!' Or for the teen behind the sound desk: 'You are brilliant with the PowerPoint – when there aren't any glitches, people really join in with the singing.' And for Harry, wearily chasing sequins across a tabletop: 'Your doing the cleaning up frees me to spend time with the parents who need a bit of TLC – thank you!'

There's more about that in session 6 of our free course (**parentingforfaith.org/course**), and a whole book on purpose included in *Parenting Children for a Life of Faith* (Omnibus).

Blessings, Becky

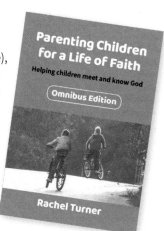

parenting for faith®

Messy Masterclasses

Could your team use a boost? We were struck by the startling revelation in Church Army's **Playfully Serious** research that only 29% of Messy Church leaders have taken part in any sort of training around faith sharing. We're now in a much better position to make really helpful training available and affordable to the network.

We are offering regular scheduled online training sessions in the most-requested and most-needed topics for training:

Starting a Messy Church

Messy Church Values

Messy Church Discipleship

You can see at a glance on our website when these are taking place across the next 6–12 months, so you can plan ahead and suggest your team books into one or more and do the training together, which is far more fun than doing it on your own.

The number of delegates per session will be limited, so the sessions can be as participative as possible. The length is a maximum of 90 minutes and they are on Zoom.

The training will be delivered by members of the talented Red team (see page 10), working in pairs to provide you with an engaging and lively session. They will not only share with you the latest developments from the horse's mouth in those different topics, but will make sure you know all the latest tools and resources available to you. They're also a great way to keep in touch with other Messy Church practitioners.

Red team logo and some of the team members

Kathy Bland

Kathy has been part of the Leominster Priory Messy Church team since 2010. She works part time for Hereford Diocese as Intergenerational Church Enabler and is a Licensed Lay Pioneer in Leominster where she also helps run the local food bank. Kathy is passionate about following Jesus to the margins and making sure faith and social action walk hand in hand.

Jane Leadbetter

Having retired from working with Lucy Moore on the Messy Church BRF team, after ten years, I am delighted to offer support to Messy Churches whilst being a busy grandparent, coordinating L19 Messy Church in South Liverpool, scouting, promoting caring for our world and making ecobricks.

Aike Kennett-Brown

Aike currently works for The Diocese of Southwark (Mission Support Officer Children and Young People). Part of her role is to champion, support and provide training for Messy Churches in that region, and to organise a biannual Messy Cathedral. Previously she started and ran a Messy Church for 7 years.

Becky May

Is a freelance writer and trainer with a heart for children, young people and families. She is part of the leadership team of Wixams Church, a Messy Church plant on a new housing development.

Cerys Hughes

I have been involved in Messy Church for around 12 years and currently work in Lichfield Diocese, enabling, supporting and encouraging Messy Church teams across North Shropshire. I am passionate about reaching

Dawn Savidge

My Messy Church journey began over 5 years ago. I have trained Messy Church leaders in lots of different aspects of MC in the North for the past few years. For my day job I am a Children, Families and Young People Advisor both locally for the Leeds Diocese and nationally for Jesus Shaped People. Feel free to contact me

Celebrating, investing and growing talents

Martin Gee, Fundraising team

This Fundraising update picks up themes from the parable of the talents from Matthew 25, which is explored in June's session material (see page 23).

Biblical talents

In the Old Testament, a talent was a unit of measurement of weight (coming in at around 34 kg). When we read about the construction of the tabernacle in Exodus 38, for example, we find that 29 talents (and change) of gold was given in offerings.

In the New Testament, the talent becomes a measurement of money instead, equating to 6,000 denarii, one denarius being the daily wage of the labourer. In today's money, a single denarius would be worth around £71.28, so 6,000 would be £427,680.

The talents given to the servants in this parable were vast sums of money. The servant entrusted with five talents had £2.1 million to manage for his master. No pressure, then…

Messy talents

As we look back over 15+ years of **Messy Church ministry**, I think we certainly see the abundant generosity of God. Whether in people giving time and energy, gifts and skills shared, answers to prayer, providential timings, encouragements and people reached, there are many reasons to be thankful. These are blessings we have seen together, including through the past months of trial and challenges. The Messy Church community has come through together, not unscathed, but also not deterred.

I very much hope that you have personally experienced something of the kindness and support of the Messy Church community in the upheaval that coronavirus brought to us all, and that you have found blessings during the challenges.

Talent givers

As I write, we are looking forward to the Messy Church Masterclass training sessions taking place in January and February, and we follow with interest the ongoing developments for young leaders sharing their experiences and encouraging one another via Zoom.

The task of the Fundraising team has been to seek funds to keep Messy Church (and BRF's other ministries) going and growing. This year, churches and donors are more financially stretched than normal, to say the least. We contacted many Messy Churches in the autumn of 2020 and explained that we were not going ahead with our annual Messy Church £100 appeal as normal, in recognition of the hard times so many were in. Despite this, a number of churches and individuals have since given, and we give huge thanks for those, and for the others who are considering giving even now.

To those who have given, prayed or advocated for BRF's Messy Church team to your churches as they consider supporting other ministries, please hear our thanks. We are working to ensure a good return on the 'talent' you have entrusted to us. We would hugely value your prayers for the whole team at BRF.

> **We would love to hear from you…** even if you just get in touch to say hi! You can contact the Fundraising team via **giving@brf. org.uk** or on 01235 462305.
>
> May the Lord bless, preserve and keep you close to him in whatever is on the path ahead.

How you can help

At no cost to you – You can support BRF through **Amazon Smile** and **Give As You Live** when you shop online. You can even raise 1.5 – 3% on your weekly supermarket shop. Details at **brf.org.uk/give**

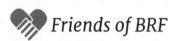

Little and often – If you can give regularly to support BRF's Messy Church ministry, it would really help, both to help us fund this ministry but also to enable better financial planning. You can become a **Friend of Messy Church** by giving as little as £2 regularly. See **brf.org.uk/friends**

Friends of BRF

Greetings cards

Following our successful launch of Christmas cards in 2020, we've started producing everyday cards which are available in packs of six. Sales of greetings cards help to fund our ministry. See **brfonline.org.uk/cards**

Session material: May 2021

Go to messychurch.org.uk/getmessymay21 to download all templates at A4 size, including a session planning sheet.

If you are using these sessions for a Messy Church at home, look out for this symbol! These are activities that can easily be adapted to the home.

Bible story

Acts 9:3–18 (NIV, abridged)

As he neared Damascus on his journey, suddenly a light from heaven flashed around him. He fell to the ground and heard a voice say to him, 'Saul, Saul, why do you persecute me?'

'Who are you, Lord?' Saul asked.

'I am Jesus, whom you are persecuting,' he replied. 'Now get up and go into the city, and you will be told what you must do.'

The men travelling with Saul stood there speechless; they heard the sound but did not see anyone. Saul got up from the ground, but when he opened his eyes he could see nothing. So they led him by the hand into Damascus. For three days he was blind, and did not eat or drink anything.

In Damascus there was a disciple named Ananias. The Lord called to him in a vision, 'Ananias!'

'Yes, Lord,' he answered.

The Lord told him, 'Go to the house of Judas on Straight Street and ask for a man from Tarsus named Saul, for he is praying. In a vision he has seen a man named Ananias come and place his hands on him to restore his sight'…

Then Ananias went to the house and entered it. Placing his hands on Saul, he said, 'Brother Saul, the Lord – Jesus, who appeared to you on the road as you were coming here – has sent me so that you may see again and be filled with the Holy Spirit.' Immediately, something like scales fell from Saul's eyes, and he could see again. He got up and was baptised.

Pointers

This month we are focusing on what is surely the most dramatic conversion story in the Bible. No one expected Saul the Pharisee to become a follower of the way of Jesus – not even the very first Christians in Jerusalem! Here was an orthodox, up-and-coming Jewish leader – one who, no doubt, had his sights set on high office – who had his world turned upside down on his way to Damascus. Everything that he thought he understood and believed was suddenly challenged and changed by his encounter with Jesus.

It makes me wonder if anyone had been praying for Saul before that life-changing day. Maybe someone in his family? Perhaps his wise teacher Gamaliel? Or was it Stephen, who perhaps caught his eye during his trial before the Sanhedrin? We know Saul was there when Stephen was stoned to death, and he would have heard Stephen say that he could see Jesus standing at the right hand of God.

This month, as part of the 'Thy Kingdom Come' initiative between Ascension Day and Pentecost, we are encouraged to pray for five other people, that their eyes might be opened to see Jesus. This story should spur us on to believe that those we pray for – even the most unlikely among them, like Saul – can be 'blinded into seeing' Jesus for themselves and become his disciples.

#discipleship: team

Messy health check

In what ways could your Messy Church be to your families like Ananias was to Saul? (Brave? Hospitable? Patient? Trusting, etc.)

Messy team theme

- Would anyone in the team like to share their story of how they came to faith in Jesus?
- Does anyone know who might have been praying for them before they became Christians?
- Who at your Messy Church are you praying for today?

How does this session help people grow in Christ?

Everyone's journey to faith in Jesus is different – only a few have as dramatic a conversion as Saul. Sometimes there may be a moment or a period of months in a person's life when everything begins to make sense; for others, the light of Jesus comes much more gradually, like a slow dawn at the break of day. However it was for you, this story encourages us to believe that God still breaks into people's lives as a result of our prayers and our faithful witness. God is already at work in the lives of Messy Church families, and we are being asked to join in with what the Spirit is doing to bring them home to God in Christ. The bright light of Jesus, which shone into Saul's life, can shine into the lives of those we meet each month. If someone as hostile as Saul can become a disciple, then any adult or child who walks through our doors this session can have their eyes opened to see themselves, others and God in a new way.

Blinded into seeing by Martyn Payne

#discipleship: families

Mealtime card

- Have you ever struggled to see something that in the end turned out to be 'staring you in the face' all along?

- Has someone ever helped you to see something for the first time?

- How might you convince someone that God is here now at the meal table with you, even though you can't see him?

Take-home idea

Search for some optical illusions online. Talk about why sometimes we can't see something that, to other people, is so obvious. Look up the illusion based on the name Jesus online (**pinterest.co.uk/pin/82612974396077940**). Can you see the word 'Jesus'? Try focusing on the spaces, not the lines. How does all this relate to the Bible story in Messy Church and how Christians believe they see Jesus?

Question to start and end the session

So… what is there around us every day that we fail to notice?

#discipleship: extra

If someone asked you to explain why you believe in an invisible God, how would you answer? Encourage everyone to have a go at doing this, using only a few sentences. Go online and find 'God Stories Today' and listen to some contemporary accounts of how people, like Saul, came to see and follow Jesus. If you were asked to share your own God story, what would you say?

Social action

Saul's conversion story was dramatic, but equally dramatic was the way Ananias dared to take a risk and welcome an enemy who had apparently become a friend. As a household, pray about how you can welcome strangers in your neighbourhood. Has someone just moved in? Is there a refugee project in your town? Does your church have a drop-in for people, where they can make friends? Work out what you could do to offer practical help and dare to make a new friend like Ananias did.

Activities

1. Stop-motion story

You will need: a camera (e.g. on a smartphone); toy or Lego pieces to represent the characters, animals and scenery in the Bible story; a well-lit corner and clear space; patience and teamwork

Create an animated video of part of today's story. Work as a team, storyboarding your film in sections, such as: the group coming up the road; the sudden bright light; Saul falling and lying on the ground; Saul listening to Jesus' voice; Saul being led into the city. Set up each scene and move the characters slowly, one move at a time. (Free stop-motion apps are available.)

Talk about what new questions and insights come to you about Saul's conversion experience, by slowing the story down and focusing on its detail.

2. Names in lights

You will need: fluorescent or shiny card; pens; scissors; glue; dark card; a large cardboard box; small torches

Jesus chose to speak to Saul in a flash of light. Both Saul's name and Jesus' name are highlighted in this story. In a bubble font, write the names 'Jesus' and 'Saul' on to fluorescent card. Cut out the letters of these names and mount them on the dark card. Put the card at the back of your box, then place

1

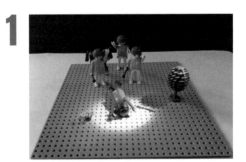

2

Session material: May 2021

the box in a dark corner. Shine your torch light on to the names to capture the dazzling moment when Jesus called Saul and Saul heard the name of Jesus.

Talk about whether you have ever heard God calling you by name. How did it feel? If this happened to you today, how would you react?

3. Flashlight messages

You will need: a strong flashlight; copies of the Morse code; pens and paper

In teams, try to read the message sent in Morse code by someone with a flashlight, who should shine the light on a dark area of your Messy Church space. Send some simple one-word messages at first, and then try longer sentences taken out of the story, e.g. 'Saul, Saul', 'I am Jesus', 'Why do you persecute me?', 'Who are you?', 'Go into the city'.

Talk about what the men with Saul thought had happened. Imagine what they said to each other later that night in their Damascus guest house.

4. A blindfold challenge

You will need: blindfolds; a variety of 'mystery' household objects

Saul couldn't see after his experience and had to trust others to look after him. It must have been very humbling for someone used to being in charge. Invite people to put on blindfolds and then present them with a series of objects. Perhaps you could include items linked to the story (e.g. a toy soldier, a torchlight, a scroll). Can they guess what they feel?

Talk about what you think Saul might have learned from this experience of being led by others that helped him become a follower of Jesus.

5. Find the Christians

You will need: sheets of A4 paper on which there is a 5 x 5 grid, labelled A to E vertically and 1 to 5 horizontally; pens and colouring pencils; something to create a barrier between two players of the game so they cannot see each other's sheets

Find and arrest five Christians hidden somewhere on the grid. Before playing in twos, choose five squares in which to write the letter C for Christian. They can be on separate squares, or in groups of two or three or more. Take it in turns to try to guess where the Christians are hiding by calling out the square reference (e.g. A4 or C3). Who can capture all five first?

Talk about why Saul was so angry with Christians. What were they saying that upset him so much?

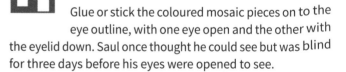

6. Mosaic eyes

You will need: sticky-back mosaic pieces; card; glue; two pictures of the human eye per person (download online) printed on to card

Glue or stick the coloured mosaic pieces on to the eye outline, with one eye open and the other with the eyelid down. Saul once thought he could see but was blind for three days before his eyes were opened to see.

3

5

6

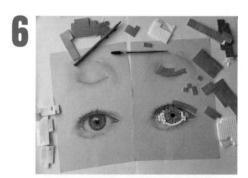

7

Blinded into seeing by Martyn Payne

Talk about why you think Saul had to wait three days before God sent Ananias to pray for him and give him back his sight.

7. Over the walls

You will need: strips of card; glue, sticky tape or staplers; string; a hole punch; a figure to represent Saul; a high place from which to lower the basket

Glue, tape or staple the strips of card together in a basket-weave design, then punch holes in the corner and thread string through each one. Draw the four corners upwards to create a basket shape, and then tie the string together. Attach more string to the hanging basket and, with your Saul figure inside, lower him successfully from a high place, representing the walls of Damascus.

Talk about why you think the Christians in Damascus decided to trust Saul and went to such lengths to try to help him.

8

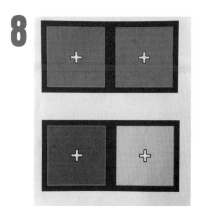

9

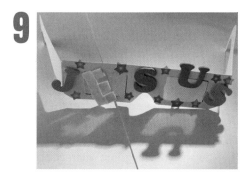

10

8. Going cross-eyed

You will need: two rectangular cards, each with two colours on them (download online)

Reddish-green and yellowish-blue are known as 'forbidden colours' – ones that our eyes (used to the normal spectrum of colour) cannot easily see. This experiment does not work with everyone first time and takes some patience. The idea is to stare at the two colours, focusing in the middle and allowing your eyes to bring the two crosses on the colours together, so that the colours are forced to merge. Many people say that they then see a new colour which is neither one nor the other, but something new. For Saul, the light of Jesus shone so bright that it enabled him eventually to see new things about himself, other people and about Jesus.

Talk about how Christians say that they live 'by faith not by sight'. What do you think they mean?

9. 3D Jesus glasses

You will need: glasses templates (download online) printed on to card; red and blue cellophane; stick-on craft letters and other decorative stickers; felt-tip pens or crayons; scissors

Cut out the glasses. Put red cellophane over the left eye space and blue over the right one. Decorate with the letters of 'JESUS' and other stickers, and colour in as you choose. Fold the sides back and wear them! Saul began to see everything differently after the light of Jesus shone into his life.

Talk about how Saul's behaviour began to change once he saw everything through the lens of Jesus.

10. Brave Ananias

You will need: 30 expendable, old playing cards; sticky white labels; pens

This is a prayer activity. On the picture or number side of the 30 cards, stick white labels. On 15 write 'friend' and on 15 write 'enemy'. Turn them all face down on the table, jumbled up. Play a game of pairs with your group, aiming to match 'friend' and 'enemy' as a pair each time. When anyone does find a pair like this, pause to pray for people who may not be our friends but for whom we can pray or maybe forgive for something they've done wrong; or even perhaps take a risk and befriend, just as Ananias did.

Talk about how praying for our enemies can often be the first step to loving them into being friends.

Session material: May 2021
Blinded into seeing by Martyn Payne

Celebration

Today's story is a journey from Jerusalem to Damascus and back again. It's also another sort of journey: a life-changing journey from darkness to light; from seein, to not seeing and then to seeing again; a journey from hatred to love. The first journey was an outward one and the second one was inward.

Let's act it out together, because this is a journey for everyone – young and old.

(*The celebration leader(s) should read out the eight-beat rhythm of the lines below which everyone should echo back along with actions as indicated.*)

(*Everyone marching*)

We're on our way to Dam-as-cus
We've lots to do; we're in a rush
For all of us; no time to rest
Saul has suspects he must arrest. Attention!

(*Everyone stop. Continue at a slightly slower rhythm.*)

But God stepped in with a bright light
It flashed around, gave Saul a fright
He tumbled down, on to the ground
And then he heard an awesome sound.

(*Everyone on the floor.*)

Leader only: Saul, Saul, why are you against me?

(*Back to call and response and the rhythm – but quieter.*)

'Who are you, Lord?' was Saul's weak cry
'It's me Je-sus,' came the reply
'Go on your way, and wait for me
Until that time, you shall not see.'

Pause. Ask these questions: I wonder how Saul felt? He had been against Jesus and now Jesus had spoken to him! He thought Jesus was dead. What must have been going through Saul's mind? Invite everyone to stand and then shuffle forward during the next part, holding out hands in front as if they can't see.

Poor blin-ded Saul, was led to town
For three dark days, was left a-lone
An-an-i-as, laid hands on Saul
His blindness went, like scales that fall.

Pause. Ask these questions: I wonder what was going through Ananias' mind? Had Jesus really spoken to him? Could Ananias trust Saul? Had Saul really changed?

With sight restored, Saul was baptised
His Christian friends were all surprised
He went a-round, a brand-new Saul
Proclaiming Christ, as Lord of all. Quick march!

(*Everyone back to a marching rhythm as soldiers.*)

We're on our way, to capture Saul
'Arrest that man', put out the call
But in the dark, he dodged them all
In a basket, down the wall.

Saul went back to Jerusalem a changed person. He had met with Jesus and his life would never be the same again. Saul went on to become one of the most famous followers of Jesus in his day and we can still read the many letters that he wrote which helped more people to find God's love for themselves.

Prayer

Seeing and not seeing are at the heart of today's story. For the prayer below, invite everyone to follow the actions before each line of the prayer:

(*Point to your eyes*) Thank you, Lord God, for the gift of being able to see the beauty of your world and each other.

(*Put your hands over your eyes*) Forgive us, Lord, for failing to see so much because of our own selfishness, stubbornness and short-sightedness.

(*Open your eyes wide and put your hands out in front*) Open our eyes, Lord Jesus, to see you at work around us in the lives of our friends, family and neighbours.

(*Shade your eyes with your hands*) By your Holy Spirit, help us to see beyond our normal eyesight so that we see the world and each other as you do.

(*Put your hands up to your eyes like a pair of binoculars*) And help us to look out for you and your kingdom wherever we go this coming month.

Song suggestions

'Why is it me?' – Alan Price (Kidsource)
'Put your hand in the hand' – Gene MacLellen (Junior Praise)
'Light of the world' – Matt Redman
'Shine a light' (Elevation Worship)

Meal suggestion

Can you add a superfood element to your main meal today? You could include some fish in your meal, because it says in the story that 'something like scales fell from Saul's eyes'.

Session material: June 2021
Don't bury your talents by Leyla Wagner and Marty Drake

Go to messychurch.org.uk/getmessymay21 to download all templates at A4 size, including a session planning sheet.

If you are using these sessions for a Messy Church at home, look out for this symbol! These are activities that can easily be adapted to the home.

Bible story

Matthew 25:14–30 (CEB)

The kingdom of heaven is like a man who was leaving on a trip. He called his servants and handed his possessions over to them. To one he gave five valuable coins and to another he gave two, and to another he gave one. He gave to each servant according to that servant's ability. Then he left on his journey.

After the man left, the servant who had five valuable coins took them and went to work doing business with them. He gained five more. In the same way, the one who had two valuable coins gained two more. But the servant who had received the one valuable coin dug a hole in the ground and buried his master's money.

Now after a long time the master of those servants returned and settled accounts with them. The one who had received five valuable coins came forward with five additional coins. He said, 'Master, you gave me five valuable coins. Look, I've gained five more.'

His master replied, 'Excellent! You are a good and faithful servant! You've been faithful over a little. I'll put you in charge of much. Come, celebrate with me.'

The second servant also came forward and said, 'Master, you gave me two valuable coins. Look, I've gained two more.'

His master replied, 'Well done! You are a good and faithful servant. You've been faithful over a little. I'll put you in charge of much. Come, celebrate with me.'

Now the one who had received one valuable coin came and said, 'Master, I knew that you are a hard man. You harvest grain where you haven't sown. You gather crops where you haven't spread seed. So I was afraid. And I hid my valuable coin in the ground. Here, you have what's yours.'

His master replied, 'You evil and lazy servant! You knew that I harvest grain where I haven't sown and that I gather crops where I haven't spread seed? In that case, you should have turned my money over to the bankers so that when I returned, you could give me what belonged to me with interest. Therefore, take from him the valuable coin and give it to the one who has ten coins. Those who have much will receive more, and they will have more than they need. But as for those who don't have much, even the little bit they have will be taken away from them. Now take the worthless servant and throw him out into the farthest darkness.'

People there will be weeping and grinding their teeth.

Pointers

A rich man entrusts his workers with his money while he goes on a trip. Two of the workers put the money to work and earn twice what they were given. When the rich man returns and sees they have doubled the money that they were responsible for, the rich man deems them 'good and faithful servants', but the third worker buried the money in the ground because he feared the man. The rich man calls him a lazy man.

- This parable teaches us that God has given all of us special gifts and talents and wants us to use them. The more we use them, the more our talents will grow.

- Jesus wants us to take a risk and use our talents, not bury them. When we unbury our gifts and use them in a positive way, we honour God.

- God gives us talents that are unique to us. It doesn't matter if we have one or ten, or if they are large or small – all gifts are important.

- We can all grow our gifts, no matter what they are. What is most important is not what our gifts are or how many we have, but that we focus on using them for the good of the kingdom.

#discipleship: team

Messy health check

Before you plan today, whizz round the team and say what everyone thinks is each team member's biggest gift. Thank God for each other.

Messy team theme

- What is a talent you have? How do you share that talent with others?

- Have you buried your talents, or are you using them?

- Is fear keeping you from taking a risk and using a talent you've been given?

- How have you been blessed by the talents of someone else?

Additional copies can be purchased at **brfonline.org.uk/getmessymay21** or using the order form on page 39.

Session material: June 2021

How does this session help people grow in Christ?

This session helps us to recognise the gifts God has given us and also recognise the gifts God has given others. It teaches us to honour God by taking risks and using the gifts we've been given instead of burying them away like the last servant. This session teaches us to trust that God has given each of us exactly what we need to carry out God's work. Lastly, this session gives us an example of what it looks like to be a good and faithful servant by loving God and others, sharing our resources and using our talents for good and for the kingdom of God.

#discipleship: families

Mealtime card

- What is your God-given superpower and how do you use it to bring joy to others?
- How do you know what ability or abilities God has given you to use?
- What gifts has someone shared with you to make your life better?

Take-home idea

This month at home, encourage, compliment and celebrate family members when you notice something special about them. Remind them that God has given them that special ability.

God, we give thanks for the special gifts you have given each one of us. Help us to always encourage others when we see them using their gifts, and help us to be brave and use our gifts instead of burying them away. Amen

Question to start and end the session

So… what special talents has God given you?

#discipleship: extra

Get together with another family and retell the parable of the talents. Talk about and celebrate each other's gifts.

Social action

Celebrate the gifts of first responders in your community by writing cards to thank them for sharing their gifts that keep you and your neighbours safe and healthy.

Activities

1. Talented people

You will need: large poster paper; marker pens

Create a group acrostic poster of people's individual talents. Write the word 'talents' vertically, leaving space between each letter. Hang the poster on the wall. Each person adds their talents to the poster.

Talk about how we all have different abilities. It is more important to use them for God than to compare them with others. How can you use your special gift for others?

2. Money bag and coins

You will need: felt or muslin; a hole punch; wool; large needles or masking tape; clay; toothpicks; scissors

Cut circles out of the material. Punch holes around the edge of the material. Weave the wool through the holes, using needles or masking tape wrapped on the end of the wool. Give a small amount of clay to make three coins to go with the money bag. Use toothpicks to decorate the coins. The clay will dry hard over time.

Don't bury your talents by Leyla Wagner and Marty Drake

Talk about how God is generous and gives us things to watch over. It doesn't matter if you've been given one gift or ten gifts; what matters is that you use your gifts and share them with others so you don't lose them.

3. Hidden talents

You will need: balloons; water bottles; bicarbonate of soda; vinegar; spoons; a funnel

Using the funnel, prepare balloons by filling each one with a teaspoon of bicarbonate of soda. It is important that the balloon looks empty; it represents our hidden talents. Fill your water bottle with a small amount of vinegar. Carefully attach the balloon to the neck of the bottle so it is hanging loosely to the side. This represents the hidden gift. Tip up the balloon so that the bicarbonate of soda flows into the vinegar. Watch the balloon inflate. This represents the found talent growing.

Talk about how God gave us special and amazing talents and sometimes only you and God know they are there and when you unbury your talents and use them they will continue to grow.

4. Risky business

You will need: small sweets or chocolates; a coin

Give a set amount of chocolate or sweets to each player. They must decide if they want to flip a coin or not. If they choose to flip a coin, heads double your sweets; if it's tails, they have to give up two sweets. If they choose not to flip a coin, they don't gain or lose any of their sweets.

Talk about how the great tragedy in this story is not that the servant didn't make more money, but that he didn't take a risk with the talent he was given.

5. Give and get more

You will need: a square or rectangular piece of paper for each person; scissors

Take a piece of paper and count the (four) corners. Carefully cut off one corner with scissors and give the corner to someone. Count the corners on the paper again. There will now be five. Repeat with each of the four original corners. Each time they give one away, they will gain one more. Share that sometimes we try to keep things for ourselves, but when we give what God has given us, he gives more.

Talk about how God wants us to not hold on tight to our gifts and talents but to share them with others. When we do this we are honouring God.

6. Using your gifts

You will need: random items that represent props that can be used for gifts or talents (for example, ballet shoes – dancer; stethoscope – doctor; spatula – chef; Bible – sharing God's stories; beaker – scientist; wood – builder)

Hide the items and have participants find them. When items are brought back, ask each person how the item could be used with someone's gift. For example, 'How might someone use their gift with the Bible?' or, 'What would someone with a gift of cooking use?'

Talk about how everyone has a gift and that God wants us to use our gifts all the time and everywhere. How do you use the gifts you've been given? Are there people who encourage you, or items that help you, to share your gifts?

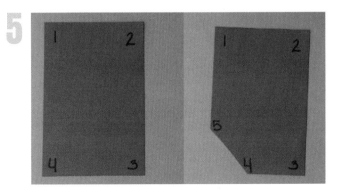

Additional copies can be purchased at **brfonline.org.uk/getmessymay21** or using the order form on page 39.

Session material: June 2021

7. Gifts and gratitude

You will need: a large piece of paper; marker pens; sticky notes (optional)

Hang a large piece of paper on a wall or lay it on a table. Write on the top of the paper, 'We give thanks for these people and the gifts they share.' Participants come to the prayer station and think about someone they know who shares gifts with them or others. Have them write the name of the person and the gift they share on the paper (or the sticky note and attach to the paper). This can be taken to the celebration and used during the prayer time.

Talk about how God gives each of us gifts or talents. Recognising and celebrating the gifts of others can be a gift! How do others use their gifts to bring you joy? Use the gift of prayer and give thanks for that person and the gift they share.

8. Share, save and spend jars

You will need: three jars or containers per person; marker pens; tags or labels to decorate; decorative items (such as stickers, jewels, paint, tissue paper, ribbon)

Give each person three jars or containers (they do not have to match). Let them decorate their jars with markers or decorative items. Label one jar 'Share', one jar 'Save' and one jar 'Spend'. Give each person ten coins. Have them put one coin in the 'Share' jar and divide the rest however they wish between the 'Save' and 'Spend' jars.

Talk about how the talents in this parable referred to a lot of money. Today we think of talents as gifts we've been given by God. This parable gives us an example of how to be a good and faithful servant by using our gifts for the kingdom of God and sharing the resources God has given us. Where will you share your resources? Perhaps with a favourite charity or with Messy Church?

9. Buried treasure

You will need: crumbly biscuits; chocolate coins; bowls; spoons

Unwrap the chocolate coins and place them in your bowl. Crumble the biscuits on top of the coins (sand). Use the spoon to dig up the coins.

Talk about how we sometimes bury our gifts inside and keep them hidden because we are afraid. When we unbury our gifts and invest ourselves in the world, we honour God.

10. Growing God's gifts

You will need: a shallow dish or cake tin; a clean, dry tin or jar; food colouring; bicarbonate of soda; washing-up liquid; vinegar; a measuring cup and spoons

Place the tin in the centre of the shallow dish. Fill the tin about ¾ full of water. Add 2 tbsp of bicarb, a few drops of washing-up liquid and food colouring. Give each person a measuring cup with vinegar in it. Slowly pour a little bit of vinegar into the jar and watch what happens. Continue to pour small amounts into the jar. You should continue to get more reactions.

Talk about how the vinegar is like a gift and, when you use it, it grows and grows. God has given each of us at least one special gift. When we use what we've been given, instead of hiding it away, we are given more.

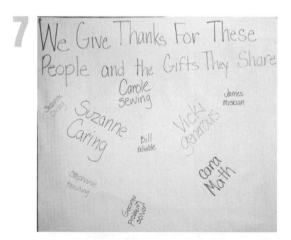

Don't bury your talents by Leyla Wagner and Marty Drake

Celebration

As you tell the story, encourage people to participate by doing the actions indicated.

Today, we've been exploring the parable of the talents. A parable is a story from a long time ago that teaches us a lesson. This story starts with a rich man getting ready to go on a trip (*walking motion*). Before he left, he decided to give each of his servants some of his possessions to care for while he was gone. The rich man gave his first servant five coins (*cheering*). He gave his second servant two coins (*cheering*) and he gave his third servant one coin (*cheering*). Even though he gave each of the servants different amounts of coins, all the coins were important!

After the rich man left (*walking motion*), his first servant went to work doing business with his five coins and earned five more (*cheering*). The second servant did much the same: he went to work and quickly earned two more coins (*cheering*). The third servant decided to dig a hole in the ground and bury his coin for safe keeping (*gasp in surprise*).

After some time, the rich man returned from his trip (*walking motion*) and went to see his servants and collect his coins. The first servant gave him the five coins he had been given and the five more that he had earned. The rich man was so happy

he called him a 'good and faithful servant' and decided he did such a good job with a few coins that he would give him much more responsibility! He invited the servant to come and celebrate (*chant 'Party, party'*)!

Next, the second servant gave him the two coins he had been given and the two more he had earned. The rich man was so happy he called him a 'good and faithful servant' and decided he did such a good job with a few coins that he would give him more responsibility! He invited the servant to come and celebrate (*chant 'Party, party'*)!

Finally, the third servant approached and said, 'I know you are a stern man and I was afraid to risk losing your coin, so I buried it.' He gave the rich man his one coin. The rich man was very angry! He said, 'My first servant gave me five extra coins, my second servant gave me two extra coins, but you were lazy. You could have at least taken it to the bank and earned some interest! You will not be celebrating with us AND I am going to take your one coin and give it to my faithful servant who already has ten' (*gasp in surprise*).

Just like in this story, God gives everyone different talents and gifts. All of them are important and God wants us to use and grow those talents and gifts to do good work in the world (*cheering*). If we don't use our gifts and hide them away, we sometimes lose them, like the third servant who buried his coins.

I wonder what talents God has given you. I wonder how you can use those gifts to do good in the world.

Prayer

Bring in the prayer station poster from activity 7 (Gifts and gratitude) to hang during the celebration. You might choose to mention how these people have shared their gifts and made the world better before you begin your prayer. Explain before the prayer that when you pause, everyone is invited to share at the same time what their gift is.

Dear loving and gracious God, thank you for giving each one of us a special gift or ability. We celebrate and give thanks for all the people who use their gifts to make our world a better place. Thank you, God, for giving me the gift of… (*pause for answers*). Help me to always use and grow my gifts so that I can share them with others. Amen

Song suggestions
'No greater love' – LifeTree Kids
'We all have gifts to share' – Susan Kay Watts
'Talents and treasures' – Joe and Tracey Cruz

Meal suggestion
Talent soup, aka vegetable soup, and grilled cheese sandwiches, apple slices and cookies.

9

10

Session material: July 2021

Go to **messychurch.org.uk/getmessymay21** to download all templates at A4 size, including a session planning sheet.

If you are using these sessions for a Messy Church at home, look out for this symbol! These are activities that can easily be adapted to the home.

Bible story

Mark 10:17–27 (NIV)

As Jesus started on his way, a man ran up to him and fell on his knees before him. 'Good teacher,' he asked, 'what must I do to inherit eternal life?'

'Why do you call me good?' Jesus answered. 'No one is good – except God alone. You know the commandments: "You shall not murder, you shall not commit adultery, you shall not steal, you shall not give false testimony, you shall not defraud, honour your father and mother."'

'Teacher,' he declared, 'all these I have kept since I was a boy.'

Jesus looked at him and loved him. 'One thing you lack,' he said. 'Go, sell everything you have and give to the poor, and you will have treasure in heaven. Then come, follow me.'

At this the man's face fell. He went away sad, because he had great wealth.

Jesus looked round and said to his disciples, 'How hard it is for the rich to enter the kingdom of God!'

The disciples were amazed at his words. But Jesus said again, 'Children, how hard it is to enter the kingdom of God! It is easier for a camel to go through the eye of a needle than for someone who is rich to enter the kingdom of God.'

The disciples were even more amazed, and said to each other, 'Who then can be saved?'

Jesus looked at them and said, 'With man this is impossible, but not with God; all things are possible with God.'

Pointers

Like many good people, the young man followed God's commandments. Jesus loved him and asked him to look deeply at those things that were precious to him and Jesus asked him to give them up, sell everything he owned and give the money to the poor and then come and follow Jesus.

Jesus said, 'No one is good except for God.'

The young man walked away sad, as he had great wealth.

Jesus said that it is hard for the rich to enter the kingdom of God, like getting a camel through the eye of a needle.

Why were the disciples amazed at these comments about rich people? Did they think that rich people were better than poor people?

Jesus said with God all things are possible.

#discipleship: team

Messy health check

What one thing could you do in your next Messy Church session to help people enter the kingdom of heaven during it?

Messy team theme

- Ask each of the team members to tell about something that is precious to them and why it is precious.
- How has Jesus asked you to step out of your comfort zone? Give an example.

How does this session help people grow in Christ?

In this story, Jesus asked the young man to really evaluate his life. What are the things that we feel are very important and valued in heaven? Do the things we feel are important bring us peace, joy and happiness? Jesus challenges us to overcome our fears and engage in the world rather than to stay protected with our possessions.

#discipleship: families

Mealtime card

- Do you think the young man eventually sold all he had, gave the money to the poor and joined Jesus?
- Jesus asked the young man to follow him. How do we, who come to Messy Church, follow Jesus?

Take-home idea

Take paper, scissors, a pencil and ruler to a friend's house and ask if they can fit through a hole in this paper? Follow the Eye of the Needle Paper Challenge (see activity 10). If they like the challenge, invite them to Messy Church.

Question to start and end the session

So… if Jesus asked, would you sell all you own and give the money to the poor?

The rich young ruler by Mark and Jane Hird-Rutter

#discipleship: extra

Organise a garage sale with a group of friends and raise money for charity.

Social action

Our society is very rich compared to others. How can we help people in these societies? Consider giving gifts to people in other countries such as through Plan International or Kiva.

Activities

1. The kingdom of heaven

You will need: small canvases; acrylic paint; paint brushes; palettes; water

Create a painting of what you think heaven would look like. It could be abstract or realistic. Before you start to paint, quieten your mind and pray.

Talk about what you think heaven is like. None of us really knows what it is like in heaven. Can we even imagine it? Let your imagination play out on the canvas.

2. How rich are we?

You will need: magazines with pictures or online pictures of poorer countries and homeless people, alongside pictures of your own country and affluent living; glue; felt-tip pens; coloured paper; scissors

Make a collage of the pictures, cut from the magazines, and then compare them to pictures of where we live.

Talk about how our world seems full of people who judge each other. Some people judge without even getting to know the other person first. God knows us all. He does not measure success, wealth or conditions. He looks at our heart. What will he see in your heart?

3. The eye of the needle

You will need: a large cardboard box; toy cars; large pieces of card; camel clip art (from the internet); masking tape; racing track or cardboard channel

Work together to create a racetrack for your toy cars. In the cardboard box create a rectangle that is 5 by 15 cm. Decorate the cardboard box and add the title, 'Eye of the Needle'. Print out the clip-art camel on the card and then fold it in two (like a tent). Take two toy cars and, using masking tape, tape the camel to the cars so that it looks like the camel has wheels. Create a track using whatever you can and try to get the camel to drive down the track and through the eye of the needle.

Talk about what Jesus meant when he said, 'It is easier for a camel to go through the eye of the needle than for someone who is rich to enter the kingdom of God.' The eye of the needle was a special gate that had a small door in it. When the big gate was closed for security reasons, the little gate could be opened. The only way to get a camel through was to unload the camel and have it crawl through on its knees (I'm not sure how that works for a camel). If we rich people unburden ourselves and humble ourselves, then we can enter the kingdom of God.

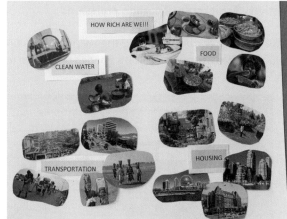

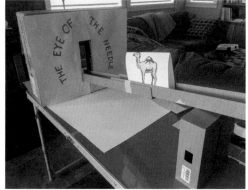

Session material: July 2021

4. Climate research

You will need: access to a computer and the internet; word-processing software and spreadsheet software; Canada's carbon footprint PDF (download online)

You might like to ask people to do this activity before your session. Using the statistics in the PDF as an example, research the same data for your country. Should you have the same categories or different ones? Using the internet, find out from your government sources how many gigatons of CO_2 your country is creating for each category and create three pages like those in the downloadable PDF.

For an extension of this activity, people could put together a large poster on a display board showing climate issues in your country.

Talk about how your country is working to reduce its greenhouse gas (GHG) production. How are you, as individuals, helping to reduce it as well? Was the data you needed easily available? How will not acting on our carbon production affect the rich, the poor, the biosphere?

5. Climate burdens

You will need: a piece of plywood approximately 60 by 90 cm; six plastic plant pots; a small plant pot filled with small polished rocks or plastic coins; sticky tape; the statistics found in activity 4; pictures of carbon emissions

Create a voting booth by placing the six plant pots on the plywood so they can all be seen. It's good to tape them to the plywood. Stick pictures to each plant pot to represent the different areas that contribute to your carbon footprint. People can look at the pictures and take a rock, or coin, and vote for which category they think makes the most carbon emissions in their country. At the end of each vote or at the celebration time, bring out the pie chart from activity 4 so people can see which is the biggest producer for your country.

Talk about how our lifestyle is putting a great burden on our planet. How can we unburden ourselves to help reduce our personal carbon emissions? What are the most effective steps we can take? The website **drawdown.org** has many answers to this question.

6. Rich man's maze

You will need: printouts of the maze PDF (download online); pens, pencils or felt-tip pens

Find your way through the maze. The answers to the questions below may be found along the way.

Talk about what the rich young man has to give up in order to get to heaven. What does the rich young ruler have to start doing to get into heaven? Are there some things that you might need to give up? Some answers can be found to these questions by following the maze.

8

5

7

9

The rich young ruler by Mark and Jane Hird-Rutter

7. Walking stick

You will need: branches of up to 2 metres in length and 2 cm diameter; sandpaper; penknives; a hand saw; paracord; scissors; a lighter; instructions (download online)

Using the saw, cut a branch so that it will be appropriate for each person. Peel the bark from the branch using the penknife (supervise carefully). If you pre-score the bark with a knife, then the bark is easy to take off. Sand any rough spots and the ends of the branch. Follow the PDF instructions for creating a handle.

Talk about how, if you wanted to walk away from God, a good walking stick would come in handy. What do you think it would feel like to walk away from Jesus? How do you think the young ruler felt?

8. The rich man's purse

You will need: chocolate coins; felt; scissors; white glue (PVA) or sewing kit; foam strips; a stapler

Cut the felt material into a purse shape and sew or glue the edges to create a purse. Use the foam strip to make a handle and staple the handle to the purse. Give each participant five chocolate coins and then have them give all the coins away. They are not allowed to eat any themselves. Chocolate coins could be replaced by real coins.

Talk about what it is like to give all your coins away and not keep a single one for yourself. Did other people like getting your coins? Did they eat them?

9. Closer to God

You will need: templates printed on to white card (download online) or plain card for people to write their own; white glue (PVA) or a glue stick; sticky tape; marker pens; stickers and pictures

Make a card with the front saying, 'What must I do to get closer to God?' and decorate the front cover with marker pens. Inside, write words that help us get closer, such as 'Love, pray, be kind, listen and help others'. Decorate with other words, pictures or stickers that might help you get closer to God.

Talk about how important it is to be closer to God. God is always close to us, but we sometimes lose touch. We need to work to keep our focus in order for us to allow God to come close to us regularly.

10. Eye of the needle paper challenge

You will need: sheets of paper; scissors; instructions (download online)

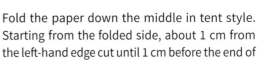

Fold the paper down the middle in tent style. Starting from the folded side, about 1 cm from the left-hand edge cut until 1 cm before the end of the paper. Turn the paper around and cut from the open side, 1 cm from the last cut and cut until 1 cm from the fold. Keep repeating this until the end of the paper. Once this is finished, there should be a series of loops along the folded edge. Cut all of these except the first and last loop. The paper should open up into a large loop.

Talk about Jesus said, 'It is easier for a camel to go through the eye of a needle than for someone who is rich to enter the kingdom of God.' Can you fit through this sheet of paper? With some careful planning and scissors, it is possible. With God's help everything is possible.

Celebration

One time when Jesus was walking with his disciples, a young man came up to Jesus and said, 'Teacher, what must I do to inherit eternal life?' The young man was dressed in very expensive clothing and Jesus thought he must be very rich. Jesus asked the young man if he knew the commandments and if he followed them. The rich young man said, 'All of these I have kept since I was a boy.'

Jesus has a very good sense of people and he often likes to challenge us by asking us to step out of our comfort zone. For instance, if someone has trouble with public speaking, he might ask them to become a teacher. Jesus looked at the rich young man and loved him. 'One thing you lack,' he said. 'Go, sell everything you have and give to the poor, and you will have treasure in heaven. Then come, follow me.'

Well, the rich young man thought this was too hard, and he went away with a sad face. Jesus said, 'Children, how hard it is to enter the kingdom of God! It is easier for a camel to go through the eye of a needle than for someone who is rich to enter the kingdom of God.'

The disciples asked, 'If rich people cannot get into heaven, then who can?' Jesus replied, 'With man this is impossible, but not with God; all things are possible with God.'

Session material: July 2021
The rich young ruler by Mark and Jane Hird-Rutter

Here are some questions to discuss together.

This rich young man wanted to be granted a place in heaven and eternal life. What laws did he follow?
Answer: The ten commandments. *Talk about what people know or remember of the ten commandments.* Most people follow these rules. Some are easy and some are harder.

Have you ever become angry with your parents?
Talk about it. How did you feel?

Have you ever made a statue of another god?
Some people say the pursuit of money is like worshipping another god.

Have you ever told lies about others?
Discuss this sensitively.

The rich man said that he had followed all of these things since he was young. He asked what else he could do to enter the kingdom of heaven.

Jesus could tell this young man was rich. He said to him, 'Why don't you sell everything that you own and give the money to the poor? Then come and follow me.' The man became troubled and walked away.

How rich would this man be compared to you? Nobody in Jesus' community would have had a house with hot water, multiple bedrooms and bathrooms or electric lights. Nor a TV or computer, or a car, health centres, or clothing as fine as is available now. No bed as comfortable. In the western world, most of us are much richer than anyone in Jesus' time.

What would it be like to sell or lose all your stuff? How long would it take to get over it? How would you manage?

Jesus then said, 'It is harder for a rich man to get into heaven than it is for a camel to pass through the eye of a needle.'

There are two interpretations of this statement. One is the Greek word *kamilos*, meaning rope or cable. This interpretation would mean it is impossible for a rich man to get into the kingdom of heaven because a cable would never fit through the eye of a needle.

Another interpretation refers to a gate called the 'Eye of the Needle', claimed to be in Jerusalem. When the large gate was closed, after nightfall, this small gate would be opened to let latecomers in. The similar word *kamêlos*, which means 'camel', referred to a real camel. The only way a camel could get through the smaller gate would be to remove its baggage and walk on its knees.

So a rich man could get into heaven if he removed his baggage and went with humility.

Which interpretation do you like best and why?

At the end of the story, the young man walked away. What do you think happened to him? Did his contact with Jesus change his life?

Prayer
Loving Jesus, thank you for all of the gifts you have given to us. We especially thank you for all of the people in our lives: our families, our friends and other people that we meet. Help us to care for, love and respect them. Help us to be kind, caring and thoughtful with them. Let us remember the rich young ruler, who cared so much for his possessions, and remind us to share with and help others. Thank you for loving us and helping us to care for others. Amen

Song suggestions
'Make me a channel of your peace' – St Francis
'Praise God from whom all blessings flow' – Thomas Ken
'I am the light of the world'

Meal suggestion
Salmon quiche and green salad. Ice-cream sundaes for dessert.

Session material: August 2021
Two by two by Sharon Sampson

Go to **messychurch.org.uk/getmessymay21** to download all templates at A4 size, including a session planning sheet.

If you are using these sessions for a Messy Church at home, look out for this symbol! These are activities that can easily be adapted to the home.

Bible story

Genesis 6:5–8 (NIV)

The Lord saw how great the wickedness of the human race had become on the earth, and that every inclination of the thoughts of the human heart was only evil all the time. The Lord regretted that he had made human beings on the earth, and his heart was deeply troubled. So the Lord said, 'I will wipe from the face of the earth the human race I have created – and with them the animals, the birds and the creatures that move along the ground – for I regret that I have made them.' But Noah found favour in the eyes of the Lord.

Pointers

When you read this, did it strike you how it could have been written for today? It did me!

We are rapidly destroying the earth that God lovingly designed and created, stripping it of its natural resources and replacing them with mountains of rubbish and pollutants, but what probably grieves God more is the way we treat each other – with selfishness and greed.

When God created our world, he declared that 'it was good', and yet people behaved so badly that our creator wished he had never made them. How bad it must have become! I wonder if he feels that way again.

The right response to human wickedness is punishment but God's wrath was not immediate, heartless or detached. It took Noah a long time to build the boat. I can imagine God grieving all that time and hoping that people would change their ways so he could change his plans. They didn't! The flood was a mighty demonstration of his power, but also of his tremendous grief.

When I read the Noah story, I see it as a wake-up call, a chance for us to restore the world to the paradise God created.

It might feel an overwhelming task, but remember Noah knew nothing about building boats when he built an ocean liner. With God in our corner, we can achieve anything. And God has a rainbow waiting for us!

#discipleship: team

Messy health check

Share one idea each about how your Messy Church is like Noah's ark.

Messy team theme

- Has God given you a new start in your life? Can you share this with our Messy families?
- Who would you take on the ark with you, given the choice, and why?
- What could you do to help God's creation?

How does this session help people grow in Christ?

It is easy to think of the Noah story as one of those 'Old Testament favourites' with little relevance to today and no connection to Jesus, but you don't need to delve far to find those links. In the Noah story, God grieved over his people, delivered justice through the flood and provided grace for Noah and his family. In the same way, God grieves over us, delivered justice through his Son on the cross and through God's grace we are all saved. But that does not mean that we should sit back on our laurels and do nothing. There is a world that needs saving too!

#discipleship: families

Mealtime card

- If you were on the ark, which animals would you like to look after?
- Which animal are you most like?
- What could you do to help God's planet?

Take-home idea

Build a house or shelter for some wildlife in your garden, perhaps a bird house or a pond.

Question to start and end the session

So… how can we make a new start?

Session material: August 2021

#discipleship: extra

Would Noah have saved more people if he had room on the ark? Think of a family that you could invite to Messy Church.

Social action

Is there an animal charity nearby, that you can help or visit?

Activities

1. Build an ark

You will need: big cardboard boxes; parcel tape; bread knife (adult to use); marker pens; blue material to lay around the outside (careful of trip hazard); big soft toy animals

Construct a giant boat that people can play in. Bread knives are great for making port holes, but be careful not to leave it lying around. Encourage people to draw waves and fish on the outside, and animals and people on the inside. An easy alternative would be two long tables laid down on their sides, with legs tied together for safety.

Talk about what it must have been like to live on the ark with all those smelly animals for a whole year. How did Noah stop them killing each other? Do you think God helped? Did they hibernate?

2. Water play

You will need: a big tray filled with water; large toy boats; toy people; toy fish and sea creatures; toy animals to put in the boat; towels

Place the tray on the floor and let people have fun playing with it. You might want to help people act out the story using the toys. Young and old alike can enjoy this activity!

Talk about how Noah's ark was a very big boat. Can you imagine trying to fit two of all the animals and herding them into their own apartments? Do you think God helped Noah?

3. Shaving foam rain clouds

You will need: shaving foam; glass or jam jar; blue liquid food colouring; pipettes

Fill the glass or jam jar ¾ with water. Spray about 2 cm of foam on top. Drip blue food colouring on to the foam. After a while, it will soak through and start to 'rain' beneath the 'clouds'.

Talk about how you think Noah felt when the last clouds were finally blown away, the rain stopped falling and the sun came out.

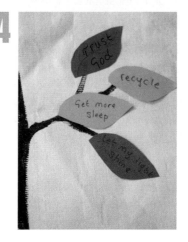

34 @MessyChurchBRF

Photocopying not permitted except under the CLA Church Licence.

Two by two by Sharon Sampson

4. Turning over a new leaf

You will need: wallpaper with a giant tree trunk and branches painted on it; paper leaves cut out (go colourful, no need to stick to green!); pens; glue or blu-tack

Write something on a leaf that you would like to do differently (e.g. let my light shine, clear clutter, get fit, waste less, drink more water, give more smiles, recycle, trust God). As you stick it on the tree, ask God to help you achieve it.

Talk about how, just as God gave Noah a new start, we can start afresh too. God will not store up the things we have done wrong. He forgives us, which wipes the slate clean, so we can start again.

5. Animal masks

You will need: thin card or paper plates; a hole punch; elastic; scissors; pens

Make an animal mask. Older children and adults might like to design their own. You could have ready-printed templates for younger children to cut and colour.

Talk about if you could be an animal, what would you choose and why?

6. Potato cakes

You will need: cooked potato (mashed); flour; bowls; cups; spoons/forks; boards; rolling pins; shape cutters; paper plates; spatula; pancake maker/hot plate; oil; butter; salt

Mix a cup of potato with a cup of flour. Turn it into dough. Roll it out. Cut out animal shapes or design your own. Fry in a little oil. Eat with butter and salt. It's as yummy as chocolate. Trust me!

Talk about if you were God and could design your own animal, what would it look like?

7. T-shirt bags

You will need: old T-shirts; sewing scissors

Turn old T-shirts into bags. Cut out the neckline, making a deep U-shape. Cut off the sleeves, just below the seam. Lay the T-shirt down and cut 10 cm strips up from the bottom of the T-shirt, about 1 cm wide. Tie a top strip to a bottom strip. Repeat all the way along. Then tie neighbouring strips together to reduce holes.

Talk about new starts. Just like Noah, these clothes can have new starts. It is good to recycle rather than throw away.

8. Rainbow paper plates

You will need: paper plates; scissors; pens or paints and paintbrushes; pencils

Draw Noah's ark and a rainbow on a paper plate, then cut out around them so that you have a silhouette. Colour them in or use paint.

Talk about how God always keeps his promises. When you see a rainbow, remember that.

Session material: August 2021

9. Pairs matching

You will need: a set of around 20 cards with pictures of animals on, containing pairs of each animal (you can find sets to print out on the internet, or make your own)

Lay the cards out face down. Take turns to pick two. If they match, keep them. If not, put them back and it's the next person's turn.

Talk about what a great variety of animals God created.

10. Concertina creations

You will need: paper; pens

Ask everyone playing to draw an animal head. Fold the paper over to hide the head, leaving two lines showing for the neck. Pass it on. Then draw the top half of the body, with arms/tentacles, etc. Fold the paper over, leaving two lines for the waist. Pass it on. Then draw the rest of the body. Fold it over. Pass it on. Reveal your creations!

Talk about how you have been as creative as God, with his giraffes, deep-sea fish and birds of paradise!

9

10

Celebration

You will need: globe; costume for Noah (if you have one); roll of paper (scroll); box of oats; animal dressing-up; water spray; things that have been made (big boat from activity 1, rainbows from activity 8); volunteers to play the narrator, God, Noah and the dove

Hide a twig somewhere in the room. Tell only the person playing the dove where it is. Act out the following script with your volunteers:

God: [*stand on a chair, holding the globe*]

Narrator: A long time ago, a very long time ago, a very, very long time ago, God looked down at the earth he had made and saw that it was full of bad people who were mean and selfish all the time. They were telling lies, hurting each other and the world, and not sharing what they had with others. This made God very sad. He was so sad that he decided to wash the earth clean with a giant flood and start all over again. But there was one man who wasn't mean or selfish. His name was Noah.

Noah: [*step into view reading a book*]

God: Noah!

Noah: [*jump, looking scared*] Sorry God. I thought you were my wife.

God: [*step down, get rid of globe, find scroll*] Noah, there is going to be a big flood. I want you to build an ark.

Noah: How will an arch help, Lord? [*hold arms up in an arch shape*]

God: Not an arch, Noah, an ark. A big boat. A very big boat. I am going to wipe the world clean. But I am going to save you and your family. Here are the instructions for how to build the ark. [*hand over scroll*] It will be 300 cubits long, 50 cubits wide and 30 cubits high.

Noah: Can you remind me how big a cubit is?

God: A cubit is the distance between your elbow and your fingertips.

Noah: Do you know what that is in metric?

God: Yes, in your case it's 41.5 cm, but since the metric system will not be thought of for thousands of years, you will have to stick with cubits. If it helps, the boat will be as long as twelve buses and as tall as a four-storey house.

Two by two by Sharon Sampson

Noah: Wow God! That is a big boat. Where shall I start?

God: You will need to [*Noah acts it out*] chop down lots of trees, cut them into planks and nail them all together. Maybe your family can help.

Noah: Can you help? [*get everyone to join in*] Chop down a tree, cut it up, nail it. Maybe the elephants could carry the trees? [*ask if anyone wants to be an elephant*]

Narrator: Finally, decades later, he had finished the ark. Phew you can stop now! I wonder why God didn't just give Noah a boat? [*pause*] Maybe because he wanted to see how much Noah trusted him, or he wanted to give bad people a chance to change. It took Noah many, many years to build the ark and all the people around probably laughed at him, [*get everyone to laugh*] but Noah trusted God and kept on going. Noah and all his family got on the ark. [*Noah and the others get in the ark*] God sent them two of every kind of land animal and bird and they went on the ark too. [*chuck in animal costumes and soft toys*] They took enough food for everyone [*hand them a box of oats*], as there were no supermarket deliveries back then, and they would be on the ark for months and months. Then God shut the door and sent the rain.

God: [*spray a fine spray over people's heads*]

Narrator: It rained for hours, it rained for days, it rained for weeks. Just imagine what it was like when it didn't stop for 40 days and 40 nights. The waters rose and rose until the ark floated. Then they carried on rising until all Noah could see was water everywhere. Because Noah had followed God's instructions the ark was perfect for the job. It floated safely on the flood and inside the ark, the animals and people were safe and dry. The Bible doesn't tell us what it was like inside the ark all that time, but I expect they were very busy keeping all the animals fed and mucked out. I expect it was quite smelly too. Or maybe God got all the animals to hibernate for a few weeks. Who knows? Eventually the rain stopped. But it took several more months for the floods to go down. One day, they felt a bump and the ark landed on the top of a mountain. Noah sent out a dove. [*Noah send out the dove*] The dove flew around, searching for somewhere to land. Eventually it came back with a freshly picked olive leaf, so Noah knew that there must be dry land somewhere. The waters carried on going down and more and more land appeared. Finally, all the people and all the animals could leave the ark. How happy they must have been and how excited, to go out into a new world and start a new adventure. [*get everyone to sit back down*]

God: Well done Noah. You have worked hard. I promise that I will never again wipe the earth clean with a flood. To remind you of my promise, I will put a rainbow in the sky. [*get those with paper plate rainbows to hold them up*]

Narrator: God had given Noah and all his family the chance to start afresh, just like he gives us that chance every day and every year. Like the people of Noah's time, we are also messing up – just look at the way we are destroying the planet God made for us. But Noah didn't have Jesus. (He lived a long time before Jesus.) When Jesus died on the cross, he took all our mistakes on his shoulders and paid the price for us. That doesn't mean that we can carry on being bad, or ruining our planet, of course we shouldn't. It just means that we don't need to worry. God won't punish us. And remember, whenever we see a rainbow or a cross, we can remember God's promise, not to flood the whole earth again.

Prayer

Let's play 'chat and catch' with God. We can chat to him and then try to catch his reply. It might be a thought or a picture, or just a feeling. He has so many ways he can speak.

Father, thank you so much for giving us this beautiful planet and all the amazing animals. Sorry that we are messing it up, not treating it as well as we could. Now in your head, chat to God and tell him your favourite animal. [*pause*] Tell God your favourite place. [*pause*] Tell God something about your favourite friend. [*pause*]

Now we will try to catch.

Ask God to show you a way that you can help his creation, making this world a better place. [*pause*] Wait for that picture or word to come into your head. [*Count to ten in your head to allow God to speak to everyone.*] Amen

Song suggestions

'The Arky Arky Song / Rise and Shine' – traditional
'Who put the colours in the rainbow?' – J A P Booth
'I can sing a rainbow' – traditional nursery rhyme
'Eye of the storm' – Ryan Stevenson
'Beautiful Day' – Jamie Grace

Meal suggestion

How about a buffet of food with animal feed labels, e.g. hay bales (bread chunks), chimp food (bananas and other fruit and veg), giraffe leaves (salad), chicken feed (crisps), panda bamboo (celery), worms (spaghetti), mice food (cheese)?

Messy questions

Richard and Kayla Harlow, with St Paul's, Tadley, Messy Church

We started to run a Messy Church in May 2015 in St Paul's Church, Tadley, UK. We've had five amazing years with about 100 people attending each month, divided equally between adults and children. As our young people have grown during those years, we noticed that their expectations had changed: they wanted more independence, more challenge and they developed new questions. We also noticed that many of our adult Messy Church members had big questions which we didn't really have time to address.

This project arose from those questions. We asked adults and young people (of all ages) to write down, totally anonymously, their 'big questions' – the questions they have about God, Jesus or the church. Some of them wrote a question to God; others wrote down something they were struggling with. We also got our 12–16-year-olds together for a focus group to hear their questions.

Kayla and I took these questions away with us on a period of study leave. We offer our responses to these questions here. We wouldn't call them 'answers' because most questions don't have neat answers and even if they did, we aren't wise enough to write them!

Jesus said, 'Ask and it will be given to you.' We believe that real questions take us deeper into God. We are so grateful for those who allowed us to see their questions. We hope that our responses will encourage you to keep asking your own questions.

We want you to be assured that our responses represent our beliefs and experience of God. They are not an official Messy Church creed or set of beliefs. As well as our thoughts, we offer some questions for you to discuss with the people around you, and an activity to take the topic further. Some of us find our answers by talking and some by doing, so pick up whatever works for you.

Perhaps you have a question you'd like someone to respond to. You could write it down and give it to whoever leads your Messy Church, or send it to messychurch@brf.org.uk.

So let's get to it, with perhaps the BIGGEST question of all:

> **God, are you real?**

A friend of mine, when somebody told him that they were an atheist (they didn't believe in God), would say, 'I don't believe in your god either.' This would surprise them, because he was a vicar!

The point he was trying to make was that people have lots of ideas about God that are so wrong that nobody wants that kind of god to be real (horrible ideas like: God punishes some people for eternity).

So what kind of god are we talking about?

Some people think that gods are superhumans (like Thor with his hammer) – bigger and stronger than us, but still locked in a struggle for the victory of good over evil. The Christian God isn't that kind of god. Gods like Thor are not big enough or strong enough.

The real God must be big enough to create the universe (and all possible universes). The universe demands an explanation: being and matter can't come from nothing, just as light can't come from darkness. Whatever created us and the universe, that is what we call God.

This is not wishful thinking. We do not just imagine such a God. Logic and science demand such a God, because nothing cannot create something. All religions and most atheists recognise this, it's just that the atheists call God something else (like chance, but chance can't create anything).

So the question becomes: what sort of god is God? Is this powerful God like us? Is this God good, kind and loving?

Not everyone thinks so. Lots of people think that the world is such a harsh place that it cannot have been made by a God who is good. But if God is not good, then how did humans develop the ability to tell good from evil? Who made us wiser (or kinder) than God?

Jesus (and the prophets before him) insisted that God is good. Jesus heals the sick, forgives the guilty, touches lepers, feeds the poor and raises the dead. He says that this shows us God. He tells us that if we have seen him, we have seen God. His life is offered as proof that God is good and God is real. You can test this proof by following Jesus: his teaching, his lifestyle. This is what Christians are doing: testing (and tasting) and seeing that God is good.

If God spoke to you, how would you know it was God?

Some people say that God didn't make a very good universe. Is it possible for God to be bad? If God is bad, then where does our sense of right and wrong come from?

Have a go at praying. Say the Lord's Prayer (Matthew 6:9–13) slowly every day for a week. See what thoughts go through your mind. This is often how God becomes real to us.